Thorpe-Bowker Publishing
First published 2024

All rights reserved.
No part of this publication may be produced,
stored in a retieval system or transmitted in
any from or by any means, electronic,
mechanical, photocopying or otherwise
without written permission of the publisher.

ISBN 978-1-7637858-16

THEY SAY
BRINGING A CHILD
INTO THE WORLD
IS A BEAUTIFUL THING
A MIRACLE,
THE GREATEST JOY...
BUT...

ARE YOU SURE YOU WANT CHILDREN?

WRITTEN BY IOANNIS

ILLUSTRATED BY MEEMEE

BUT WITH A GROWING POPULATION, THE COST OF LIVING, LOSING SEVERAL FRIENDS TO PARENTHOOD, AND THEIR LOVE OF A SINGLE, CAREFREE LIFE WITH NO DEPENDANTS, THEY ASK THE QUESTION...

DO YOU LIKE TO SLEEP IN ?

ARE YOU SURE YOU WANT CHILDREN?

DO YOU REQUIRE 'ME TIME'?

DO YOU APPRECIATE

NICE THINGS?

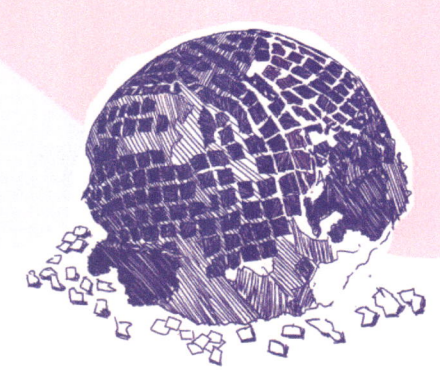

DO YOU LIKE
HAVING EXTRA MONEY
TO GO ON HOLIDAY?

DO YOU HATE MESS AND PREFER THINGS BEING IN ORDER AND TIDY?

ARE YOU SURE YOU WANT CHILDREN?

DO YOU APPRECIATE PEACE AND QUIET WHEN DRIVING?

DO YOU SAVOUR HAVING INTIMACY WITH YOUR PARTNER?

THIS BOOK IS TO BE READ IN JEST.
WE DO NOT TAKE ANY RESPONSIBILITY
FOR THIS MESSAGE ... OR FOR YOUR CHILDREN
ツ

www.ingramcontent.com/pod-product-compliance
Lightning Source LLC
Chambersburg PA
CBHW041724070526
44585CB00006B/143